MORPH BRED

Wynter Lauren Eddins

Copyright © 2016 Wynter Lauren Eddins

All rights reserved.

ISBN: 0692645373
ISBN-13: 978-0692645376

January 1st, 2016

1:43a.m.

To you,

      The one who has opened up this book, you have also opened up a piece of my heart. This collection of poems is a journey that I continually experience, the despair, the love, and the growth. To immerse myself in art is the most powerful love I ever felt. Thank you for sharing in my experiences and letting them be apart of you. You are a beautiful creature made to create. This is my creation, a color spectrum that will take you through Darkness, exploring feelings of loneliness and depression, to the purple despair called Love, and reaching the Light which dives into forgiveness, lessons learned, and ultimate transformation. I believe human beings are resilient rocks who will weather the storm, and go through the process of melting, cooling, and solidifying into their true purpose. We must embrace all personal experiences for the growth we desire. Live and survive through Darkness, Love, and Light.

Yours truly,

Wynter Eddins

I. OBSIDIAN
- Alone Inside (5)
- Dagger (6)
- Hiding Blind (7)
- Leave Alone (8)
- Pain Fest (9)
- Dead Love (10)
- Stab Back (11)
- Fell Lone (12)
- Red (13)
- Fail Ship (14)
- Stand Under (15)
- Controlum (16)
- Spin Life (17)
- Wood Monsters (18)
- Crawling Wall (19)
- Wind Sweep (20)

II. AMETHYST
- God's Price (22)
- Pass Back (23)
- Expired Wants (24)
- Enough Confusion (25)
- Submerge Me (26)
- Frame Love (27)
- Purple Soul (28)
- On the Other End (29)
- Hunt Love (30)
- Chronicle (31)
- Triumph Glimpse (32)

- Moon Tox (33)
- Why You? (34)
- Love Bind (35)
- Night Gold (36)
- Dare Fly (37)
- Caged Love (38)
- Sunk Heart (39)
- Violin Hum (40)

III. IVORY

- Martin (42)
- Devil's Sleeve (43)
- Tunnel Vision (44)
- Canto (45)
- Come Dark (46)
- Light Heal (47)
- Moon Lit (48)
- Touch Real (49)
- Love Fill (50)
- Heal Far (51)
- Simmer Soul (52)
- Mother (53)
- Stumble In (54)
- You Bye Good (55)
- Sky Truth (56)
- Above Such (57)
- Chaotic Peace (58)

ACKNOWLEDGMENTS

I would first like to thank the woman who has always believed in me, who continues to support my dream, when she has no idea what my vision entails. Thank you Mom, you are the reason I keep pushing, because you believe in all that I do. Thank you for listening to all of my poems and being the first to hear my material. Even when you were tired, you always let me express myself. Thank you to my family, my father, brothers, and sister who have always lifted me up in my times of need. I love you all.

I would also like to thank my public relations representative and friend, Chriss Ramos for supporting me in my dream and encouraging me to keep on the path of passion. Thank you to all my friends and family who have been a huge part of my creative process

Thank you to all the other artists who have shared their work openly, and have left a piece of their heart on the numerous L.A. stages. We must support one another, by doing so we will always evolve in our creative expression.

Thank you to Lorna Alkana, the illustration artist for the cover of Morph Bred. Thank you for taking the time to capture the essence from an artifact that means so much to me. Your passion for life, and the way your positivity inspires others, makes me feel blessed to be apart of your expression.

Obsidian

Even though I use to fear you, I thank you for putting me through this part of my cycle.

Darkness, I have come to know you all too well. You slept with me on my coldest nights. You promised to never let me go, even though you were sucking my life. I thank you for testing me, for putting so much pressure on me, I almost gave up. Even when I felt it was impossible to keep going, I knew you were temporary, this feeling of despair and hopelessness would pass. I use to sit with you embracing those lonely hours, rocking back and forth. I begged you to leave me, but your grasp was a clutch I could not see. I only felt the way you lingered in my thoughts, your perverseness made me not want to do anything with my life. I was ready to give in to you Darkness, I was ready to let you take over.

It was that night where everything came crashing down. When I saw that there was no turning back. Life or death, those were my only options. I chose to live. I chose to be free from you. I chose to never look back. I asked myself, "Will I live for you or will I live for me?" I chose me….and you, Darkness, I left you in that garage that cold night where you attempted to take my life, and by His grace, I escaped.

I still have scars that have healed and blistered over, plastered on my body to remind myself why I cannot ever, ever turn to you again.

Here is your tribute, and this is where I begin…DARKNES

ALONE INSIDE

No one can see what is happening inside close doors. No one can see what is going on. So things in the dark, there remains no right from wrong. No one hears the whimpers at night. It's silent outside. Not a chirp, not a sight. No one listens to the desperate heart. Calling loudly, but the night is a dart. Stabbing each time more painful then. Sitting there staring at the reflection I am in. Does anyone notice the black circles I've drawn? To point to the attention that I am alone.

DAGGER

Dagger, stop piercing. You are stronger than most. You are small, but you are sharp, and you killed all of those lonely hearts, they sit stabbed. With razor darts, that you dagger, exploded in. No permission. Only sin. Dagger, stop with your lies. Acting like you won't stab me. I know your lines. That's all you are made for is to kill and erase names. Erase hearts, and fill them with pain. I would rather live this life in vain than to let you pierce another vein. No more shame in love.

HIDING BLIND

There were times I use to be a shadow. Crawling on the walls, and through the meadows. Hiding from the shame, that came with each look. I use to be a shadow. Physical use of the body, a temple, it was destroyed because I gave the key to the wrong person. Tears have stained the window. Pain has come from time. Healing comes thereafter, but I say I am just fine. Flying faster than the wildest, I know I can escape. I have come from only greatness, and this I cannot mistake. Shame has hovered over. It passes along through. We are not here to discover who. We are here to discover truth. Lost, sometimes I feel I cannot go back. To the times that use to give me life, I wanted all of that. Pain, it was good, I use to like how it felt. But when the bruises appeared. I could no longer deal. I could no longer see. I was blinded to be. Off into the sea. I almost drowned. I was saved by my insecurities. What if I could not swim? I may have sank ten miles then. Gasping for fresh air, I look out . Then I see the faces. Friendly, they stare . What do they see? A pained spirit I use to be.

LEAVE ALONE

Leave me to die here. Alone.
That is where I feel most at
home. Leave me to wither away
in this cold. I am stuck here. And
I want to grow old in this pain. It
stains my heart, like a flame it
starts to warm me in a way.
Give me space, and let me stay
in this nothingness and this
ugliness. It makes me feel
something in this,
Cold world.

STAB BACK

Backstab why did you cut so deep? I let you stab me in my back, not to feel it in my feet. I let you get so close you drowned. In my eyes you frowned. Didn't please you to see, that I was finally becoming free. So you scarred me just to know that your love could no longer grow. You were a seasoned plant, a desert ant. You traveled looking but now you can't, bring me down to your grave. That was made the day we lay. I am climbing just to see air and you kept me way down there. Almost forgot what light looked like. Then I remembered. You were the night.

FELL LONE

I am just as lonely as they said I'd be. Alone is my own misery. And yet it seems that to others my life appears so jolly. But if they only knew where I lay my head at night, the pillow does not belong. To me or the fellow next; I do not know nor do I take the time. For it is the regular and thou are just fine. I would rather die than to see a happy flame. For in it, it would grow and then that would be to my shame. For in my darkest hour I only see the glory. Of life and life thou should live, but it is fear that rots in me. I do not see today, nor tomorrow. I only see away. My dreams are distant gallows where darkness creeps and glows. For in those deep dark shadows, my heart only knows.

RED

Red, that luscious color was so vivid. All those nights. Even when he was livid. Red eyes blasted out from his drunken highs. Red. The blood she tasted instead of his strung out kiss. He had slapped her lips. Red, the cherry lipstick smeared on her cheeks and she could not help but feel defeat. Red, the grip of his knuckles around her neck. She's almost dead. Red, he heard the sirens scream inside his head, but he refused to let her go, so his grip turned Red. His grasp finally loosened, but it's too late, she's dead.

Red.

FAIL SHIP

Give me more than what has come from this. You are sitting there, but there is more to see. Just to be inside is like a light that burns at night. Just to get a glimpse, is everything it turns to sin. I am a mere being. Hoping that I will stop seeing the negative outcome on everything. And yet I look for it. I hope it fails and it will and it shall. I have steered this ship straight down. And it will sink and I will frown. Knowing that I caused the leak. With my defeat. With my mentality. That has shaped my reality. I have built up a wall that is a hundred feet tall. And if you climb over, I will kill my only lover. You are stepping on dangerous ground. And when you enter, I will tear you down. Because you have breached a delicate crown.

Cold queen.

STAND UNDER

You wondered why my grudge cannot budge. You wonder why your words will never do. And if you even tried to take the lead. If you spoke of your dirty deeds, it would never promise you that space you want. You impostor. You fool. Whoever told you that stature is earned? And though good deed you do those dirty match your every move. Your lies will never do. They are blacker than the blackest blue. And keep on pushing through, exploiting others just for you. And if you ever tried for salvation, the book would burn your blistering hand. And you justify to everyone's eyes, but mine, for the shades you wear I can see right through. Tell me why you never told them the truth. It will catch up. And when it does, you will wish you never took from your people, your own blood. Stabbed them with your pain. Whoever knew, I could come to hate. Only You.

CONTROLUM

Mistake a man for his power, you've failed miserably. He held on to your collar, told you it was not history. You took the sweet spoon and only tasted the bitter. This man held you so tough and now your knees they do splinter. He keeps you there. Says to stay put or he solemnly swears. He will lash you like a tiger, vicious as one too. You'll end up with so many stripes. This is nothing new. So you bow down to this man, who grasp your dim light. He latches your hand. And chokes it damn tight. Squeezes it for reminder, better not break his rules. He rules his world. His world rules you. You play a part. Part's been played many times. He's a puppet master. He calls you his mime. Control me, you like it. You like being told. Got so use to it. It can never grow old. Only old you can grow, and your growth has been stole. By a man who said he loved you. A man with death's soul.

SPIN LIFE

If you just make me see something more, because clearly this is not enough. And I have been trying for so long. I don't know if there are tough times to jump over or worst times to roll under. Could the sea just pass this way today? I don't mean to stay here. I want to be washed away to a different place. Back to reality. I did not touch you because you were my gravity. A force that pulled me down so tough And now you tell me you don't want to be so rough. Now you say that we should sit and talk. That before I left, you didn't mean to bruise my walk. You didn't mean to bruise my eye and make me cry. Your aggressiveness is passive now. You did not mean to shy away from the fact that you had no mercy back then. You would have killed me that night if life did not spin.

WOOD MONSTERS

Forget that darkness will come tonight. Understand the fog comes too. Acknowledge the monster in the woods. Hear the owls crow. Forget that darkness is coming tonight. Lift your head from your knees. Embrace the withering cold. Light a fire to ease its breeze. Speak soft to Ol' boy, he lay. Silence his cowering bark. Forget the darkness has come tonight. Undo your kneaded bun. Let loose your auburn twirls. Watch the windowpanes frost bite, shiver to its patterned frame. Speak soft now to Ol' boy down there. His bark now loud and new. See slowly as that door nob turns. Lock doors will hold their stay. Let them in when fear has overcame. Your head is in dismay. Speak softly now to Ol' Boy. His worked up tag now wails. Let in the darkness that knocks. Darkness shall prevail.

CRAWLING WALL

Wallpaper has been crawling at night. They think I'm crazy, but if only they might. See my wallpaper crawling at night. It whispers things that makes me feel fright. I lay there scared, holding the covers real tight. Hearing my wallpaper crawl in the night. And in the day it always stays, but never lays in the night. And if you stay you will see too. That my wallpaper yellow really is blue. And if you wanted to see the truth, my wallpaper will you show you. But only if you hear it crawl in the night. Whispering things that makes me feel fright. Almost tore it down, but it said it might. Burn us all when it stalls in the light.

WIND SWEEP

She could have been anything with a spirit that was still burning. She could have been in the sky, soaring there and now she flies. She could have stayed in the clouds, thoughts so deep, words so loud. She could have been anything. But her voice got lost and she could not sing. Lost soul, there she goes again. Wandering aimlessly. So no one she knows. As she gives herself to anyone who will recognize that she needs to feel. Even if it is a lie, she needs to touch, even if it is too much. She has lost herself again. And no one lets her in. So she stays out in the cold, and loses all she knows. She could have been anything but the wind has swept, and she could not swing.

Amethyst

Love, there are so many sides to you. I use to only see one, and in turn I associated you with pain and misguidance. I was use to it, and I felt I deserved to feel your burn. It wasn't until I discovered the other side.

Self-love was the greatest love of all. To explore and finally recognize myself was the purest love I ever felt. God's Love. I understand it now, to love oneself and honor thyself is the greatest glory we can experience. It took me twenty plus years to understand that I no longer needed to seek love outside of my own. I could look within and fill the void I thought needed to be filled by someone other than me. Love, you grow inside now like a flower's first bloom, you are beautiful and rare. I look to you when I feel I am going astray to remind myself that you remain waiting patient for me to recognize you. Love, I thank you for not judging the wrong decisions that I have made in the past, instead you let them flourish and ground me so that I come back to you, and you accept me with open arms.

Love, you have allowed me to spread your essence around. I think you are contagious, the way you make me feel, I want others to feel this way. I want others to see the power they can have, as long as they have you. I am humbled, learning that outer "love" is temporary and cannot heal the scars within.

I have spent many nights writing about love lost, or the misperception of what love is. This tribute is for you, the good and the bad… Love.

GOD's PRICE

She could have left many years ago. Broken spirit and yet she still knows that her heart is in it. For a reason she has been with it. Over and over again she ask herself. Should I give him another year till the kids can be by themselves. She swallows her pride and closes her eyes when he walks in after night. Three hours past the light. He crawls in. And her skin crawls again, because his scent is strong of all night long. And it lingers. On linens and his fingers are cold as ice. As he brushes her back, she ask God the price she has to pay, to keep the family she prayed for each day. And the soul she sacrificed to stay. In such a dark place she lay. And he looks on like a distant song.

He sings to her of empty promises. So she hopes one day that he will be gone.

PASS BACK

My eyes fill with something, but I won't call it tears. You see, if I let my eyes know the truth, then they tell my ears. And my ears are quite sensitive, they whisper to the mind. Then all is lost, because I cannot tell the time. I am suspended in a dimension of despair. I've been trying to come back. I just don't know how to get there. You see I am stuck in a sad place, next to a rock. There's this small space of hope, but it's barely a lot. I'm searching, yearning, for something to complete. I jumped on you, and forgot to land on my feet. I'm face down, heart heavy, soul still light. I'm wondering if you'll help me get through this rite and passage me along the way. Guide me for a minute and just let me stay with you. Please don't look into my eyes. They will recognize your truth, and turn away at the sight.

EXPIRED WANTS

Lust expires. It turns into dust, but first let me speak about this lust. Tongue dripping. Pain tripping. Lust gripping my thighs. My inner ride of my life. The thrill of the night. Call it trivial, call it a sight to see, those who lust me. I cannot see them. I cannot believe them. I am them. Lusting extravagantly. Yearning for someone to see. My grip is strong but not for long. If he can't give me the love I need then I move on, to someone who can do the deed. Lusting, loving, lusting, wanting. I want you, I need you in this moment. Hold me like you own it. We don't have to be in love tonight. Just give me all you got, and that will be alright. I gave you my soul, but you let it all go. Time is up, the clock ran out. My lust has turned into a permanent drought. And I am forever lusting without.

ENOUGH CONFUSION

All the time my mind has been running for you, and yet you are running the opposite way too. I will catch up if you will slow down. But your feet are now charging and I can't cover enough ground to see you. I can't believe you would leave me in such a state of confusion, and your intrusion into my heart was unnecessary. We can part ways. Just wanted to know what you had to say. Okay, goodbye.

SUMBERGE ME

If you submerge me make it real. Hold me down until I cannot feel. Body numb, brain goes dumb again for you, and I play the fool every moment. I want you, but now you own it. Every little piece, every tiny bit. Even the microscopic atoms made of it. And you make me feel nothing. So I sit there waiting. One day I will feel something. One day I will be okay . And one day it will be my way. But the day is a distant dream. And I lean on the delusion, that we could last. It is all confusion. Why did you ask me to stay here?. Was it in fear that I would go on without you? So you want me to drown two souls who have known from the beginning. That if they last, they would never be winning. This fools game. So I take part in the blame. For dragging this along. And I am moving on to another lover. Goodbye.

FRAME LOVE

Lover stop wishing ill will upon me. I lay there with a fleeting heart, and a head that beats upon your part. So tirelessly, you have carried me in your art. I have survived in each stroke. The canvas has provoked my next move. It is retreating and now you are pleading for me to stay. I am trapped in your picture, and the frame is on its way. I must move before we reach perfection. It's a moment in time and you are my reflection. I want to burn you sometimes. Scratch between your lines. Kick you down and stomp, and say I've had enough. I do not deserve you here and now.
So farewell and it is what you have allowed.

PURPLE SOUL

Purple sheets you are so inviting. Stretching from end to end. You are thriving. Purple sheet will you warm my soul? I will place it here. I hope you will not let go. Even when the owls have gone and the crows have shown their morning wake. Purple sheets please do not take the comfort away you have provided. I will be back later to continue my hiding. Inside you. And do not turn blue when I leave for sometime. Because purple sheets you are always on my mind.

ON THE OTHER END

If I were to call you today, I wonder would you pick up. Would you hear me out, my story one more time? For in it I would tell you all that you need to be mine. And then after we would laugh about how long we've been apart. We would promise one another, that we should never again start. For misery invites company and then treats him to tea. Then when he sips she slowly takes his life away from thee. But when you pick up my call, you'll know what you have missed. For my heart, my beating soul, has wished to kiss your lips. You will hear as soon as the ding goes off on your phone. That I, your once true love still waits all alone. And if you listen close you will hear my black still heart. The one you left to die. The one you promised not to part.

HUNT LOVE

You are a mysterious fascination I've been yearning for. That's why I wait for you outside your locked door. You never did once look my way. But that intrigued me more. Prolonged my stay. A secret obsession. You were my blessing, and I was to bestow myself on your porch. I wait for you drenching wet. Rain pours out, though the month was not march. I'll be with you even if you do not want. I am the force of the love. The love of the hunt.

CHRONICLES

She sat there waiting. He would ask. He must be contemplating on whether or not she is the one. So when he entered the room, her heart soared to the sun. Five years they had been together, so it was now or never. This was the moment she had been waiting for. She read his hints. She knew what was in store. When he told her he had planned a special night. And for her to dress up, and everything else he would delight. This request made her believe in love again. Her heart almost let him go, but this night he was back in. As he approached her, she could not help but smile. Her love had shrank into an inch, but now it ran for miles. Her tears began to swell. Well, he said, the reason you are here is...His words trailed off, he lowered his head. I love you my dear but I am diagnosed to die. I am giving you all that I have until I return to the sky. And it will be faster than longer, so lets make this moment last, lets grow stronger. All night, they cried and laughed, and cried again with each other. She promised to hold on to her lover. And when he left, she never loved another.

TRIUMPH GLIMPSE

Please see me kneel. I cannot heal from the wounds. Too deep, cuts so much. I can barely stand with two feet. Joy has come. It passes on through. Then loneliness sets in, and I am no longer true to my reflection I face. And to you, I hope you chase me up mountains. And when I jump I hope you catch me. I hope you are triumph and I am faith, and when we meet we are everlasting grace. Because I saw you, just a glimpse. You peeked at me then you went somewhere. I hope you come back. So I can hold you and get back, to who I was.

MOON TOX

Isn't love just a sinner's game? Taking the love and replacing it with blame. You were a distant moon that I traveled too. Just to find out that your air was toxic. It was only doom. And you sucked me in to your gravity. I could of died with your pull. It was better to see than to feel. I should of stayed back. I should of yield. But you had already won me over. And I was sitting there, I was only over our love when it burned out. I was coming down. You were turned out. And I could see that you could see, that your love was replaced with hate for me. And when I ran you pulled me back. You grabbed me hold; you threw me at. And I almost died. I almost left. But when I turned right. I finally escaped death.

WHY YOU?

You believe me don't you? You will stand up for what is true. And why is my opinion wrong from yours? Why are you always so sure? Why can't I say what I believe, without you wearing your feelings on your sleeve? Why must I tiptoe when you are around? Why must I crawl when you walk the ground? Where do we go from here? I only exist if you come near. I can only see myself not you. I am nowhere and you are not true.

LOVE BIND

Love sometimes binds us then tears us apart. That is why I was hoping we were blind from the start. Do not worry I am staying here waiting for you. You are my true star and I am your moon. Do you need me to still shine light on your shadow? I was hoping that we would be close in this channel we call life. You were my lover. I wanted to be your wife. We were stuck in a deep blue sea, and there were sharks and monsters surrounding you and me. I will get back to shore if you'll come. But if you stay I know that I will no longer be the one.

NIGHT GOLD

I was waiting for you all day and night. I even stayed an extra hour to the next day light. You promised me you were coming. You promised me you were loving only me. I was waiting for you, though the night turned cold. I didn't budge, not a muscle because you were my gold. And I would see you real soon. That is what you said. But you never showed up and I was almost dead. When I realized you weren't coming. And I stood there; I was stunning, but you would not see. I was waiting for you, but you could not be there for me as I was for you. And I finally see. That you and me. Were never meant to be.

DARE FLY

Flying today, all the way down to the sea. I started up here in the sky, but the pain has dropped me down to my knees. And as I plead, I beg for you to see. That I am as human as you, and you are as human as me. So why do we cast each other out with each word we carry out? It is sickening to see you getting over on me. And still I want you to stay. Still I want to hold you, and I want you to play with my soul. I want to grow old in your cold. And please forgive me for staring. I don't want you to disappear. It is daring enough that you are here with me. In the midst of this stuff.

CAGED LOVE

Lover, dark lover, with hands of one another. We set still today, just looking at each other. Wondering if you find me, you'll love more. I love you still. I love you even if you will hurt me. You hurt me and yet I am here to set you free. Caged, enraged you sit there. I caress you, and you always swear that I should turn around now and go elsewhere. But I want to be here. Even if you do not want me near.

SUNK HEART

Suddenly my heart does not know it's rhythm anymore. It beats, then beats again, and then stops and feels sore. It has been through too much and it will never be enough again to pump steadily. It always heavily drags along baggage. And who would have it? They would need to carry and share me. And that will not do. Heart so sunken deep. It will never know the truth.

VIOLIN HUM

Violin hum to me again. Kiss me gently and then play with my sin. Make it feel something. Make me feel cool. Violin playing. I sit on the stool. Cold hands reaching. I always let them touch Because that violin makes me feel like I'm not doing enough. Too many chords have been moved all through my hips. Violin had me moving as those hands did their dips. And I closed my eyes. And the pain it was high. Because the violin had me feeling like my life was a lie.

Ivory

You fill me up everyday with sureness and confidence to move in my own direction.

Light, I have seen you even in the darkest times, you remain there. I use to mock my elders who said I would not be the same person from when I was younger. They told me, everyone grows, everyone changes, and if I didn't then I wasn't moving forward. I did not listen, so sure in my ways, I refused to seek change.

However, change comes when the mind does not expect it and the heart accepts it. I can say now, I am a woman, who has embraced the light and cannot turn back.

Thank you for reminding me that life is a balance, and you must exist within it. I could not have transformed without you. I still need you to remind me why I am doing this. Why I am moving the direction I am.? Your assurance comes to me in an abundance of both motivation and deliverance.

I can go on. I can survive anything. I can persist. I can endure. I can believe in this world. There is hope, because you exist.

This tribute is for you, my....Light.

MARTIN

Tomorrow I will whisper your name so that you may hear it. And the winds will carry it upon their lips. Tomorrow I will tuck your name so deep in my womb that my unborn child shall know it upon welcome. Tomorrow I will look for you just as I did today. And tomorrow, I know you will never come my way. Because death brings forth an eerie calm, so disdain, so unnatural and yet here I am, praying again to the same God, that has promised to keep you. That keeps you company since I no longer can hold your hand. Because my plan for us was broken the night you walked out. Said you were going to the store if the return policy allowed. But you never came back, two shots and there was no doubt. Taken, gone, mistaken, black hooding when they said you couldn't. Rain drops pouring, that washed away your tomorrow. Drowned out my hopes for a future to see you grow. Sorry Ma'am he's gone, they tell me with no face. I raised hell for you that day, heaven was your place. Too good for this world, that kills youth on a dime. He took you for better reasons, and forgot that you were mine. To replace you would be impossible, to start over, I can't, but I imagine you want me to smile, to live with happiness. As I know your suffering is over, and you watch down on me. Just as I watched you when you were my little baby. Forever, till we meet, I keep you in my soul. For tomorrow, I will dream of you and tomorrow son, you will know.

DEVIL SLEEVE

Give to me something that I can hold. Close to me and then we both become bold. Like the boulders that we have climbed so many times. I cannot fall down again. Tumble and frown again. I cannot give in to this place. I must find my way and stay in the right path, and laugh at those who frown at me. If I stay here, I will never be free. I must keep pushing and shoving inside of me. Nothing is settled, nothing is here in this meadow but the death that is sneaking up on all of us. And all of this stuff is nothing. It is something, only if you believe that you control what the devil has up his sleeve.

TUNNEL VISION

Visionary had tunnel vision that seem so contrary to its purpose. Narrow scope, only one focus. Route so clear and precise. But not alive, not throbbing with blind eyes. Visionary had tunnel vision, always skipping the moment, never on it, on to the next. Do what is best and you will love every minute of this stuff. You are here for a reason so don't you dare give up on what you dream of every night. It will happen with love and compassion. But also remaining in sight, and giving the light to what you desire. Live higher in Him. And do not give in to humanities cruelty. Swift hands that cause people to see that they have potential only if they can be resilient in the face of ultimate adversity. Live thoroughly and holy, and show everyone that it is you to see. You are special and you are worth it. And your love for everyone is what grows it. Give it back tenfold, expect nothing but what you hold. Your tender heart is far too bold for this cold world. So when you hide they know that at least you tried.

CANTO

Is it simple enough to say I am blessed? To understand that I too have a purpose. To know that I came with something more to offer, than a swing of my hips or the kiss of my lips. That I too, can speak the words of persuasion. That I too, can listen to the sounds of inspiration. That I too, can come to know the meaning of this world. That it offers more than such a mind can think to know. I live for these moments of creativity and time. Alone, it's okay because I can appreciate all that's fine. Everything is not in focus making life so bittersweet. Is it simple enough to know that I too can defeat? Any obstacle, any trial, I know I will get through, because being blessed, is being safe too. I can go and experience anything anywhere. To travel, even if my mind is my vacation lair. Do not think that I take this life for granted. This beauty, escapable place is under my fingertips. Do not anger when I use life to my benefit. To thrive in happiness and wander in blissfulness. Speak of me when gratefulness is due. I treasure my life and thou should you.

COME DARK

And when the shadows fell, blackness arose from the mighty pits. Calling out for the blood of the light. Damn those that cower to their knees each time darkness comes for us. For its eyes were but empty vessels. Hell had howled hypnosis upon them. Igniting the cries of deafening sound just so that darkness can prevail once more. Keeping down the souls of courage. Leverage only what darkness can allow. More have come to kneel before it not knowing their bent knees were sure to swell. Only if they looked back, towards the light. Pulling, pushing off those midnight blinders. Questioning, who is darkness? Remember the times we laughed in the light? Stop forgetting the way we held a mirror of bright. Take off your shoes that glue your feet. Understand that darkness too can be defeat. Victory lies where your dreams still exist. Work to know that happiness can persist.

LIGHT HEAL

I look for you every night without fail. I just hope you might illuminate my soul tonight. Take me up there with you, dance and be true. I love the way you look for me. You shine on my face. I am a mere being and you are my grace. I was looking for you tonight. I was hoping you might touch my heart. Heal it of indecencies if you please. I was searching for you tonight. Waited all day but then it turned night. I looked up and you were there. Clear as light. I hope you love me with all of your might.

MOONLIT

Did not mean to step in your way. Path was guided and it happened to be today. You are a constant upbringing, a reminder I'm still living as you dangle above my head. Everything I thought was a moment instead you hold me like a cloud without wings. Caressing my face, you are my everything. I look to you, just to know that your love is endless. It's like your glow that warms my soul and takes me to a better land where we are hand in hand. I dance with you until the end. And when the music stops your heart does not cease. If you could cry your tears would be a tease. A taunting sensation. I want you here to guide our translation.

TOUCH REAL

Touch me again. I know you do not love me but I will still let you in. Just touch me again. And remind me how it feels to feel what could be real. I just need you to touch me again. And stare into my eyes. And even though their lies, I will believe them in the moment. That you gave me I will own it. And I will thank you from inside that you touched me with your light. Though it will burn out tonight it is alright. I just want to feel what it feels to be almost real, but not quite. And tonight is the night where I live in your sight. I am blinded by the light. I like the way it burns me. And for the moment you can yearn me. And as it passes through like the ocean blue, I will realized I was that much closer to my truth.

LOVE FILL

Fill me up with something so pure, that when it is in my blood it feels so sure. Feel me up with love so clean, that the waters become my everything, and my thirst is quenched with His mercy. Feel me up so I can be tough and light, and I will no longer feel such demise. Though pain is still lingering in my limbs. Feel me up so that I can finally begin this journey. This beautiful journey that I have been yearning for. Dreaming about. I am here and I will no longer doubt where I will end, because right now this is where we begin.

HEAL FAR

I am farther again. I am in the distance and you are running at me with full charge and in an instant we are at one another's mercy. And it is driving me crazy. I am thirsty for the blood and if it comes I will not be able to get enough. For my tongue is forever dry, so I speak words that are always a lie. And I am alive today. Finally I can say that I can feel. And fill me up just to heal. I say thank you to mountaintops. It's where I climb and the climb does not stop. But sometimes I reach a place of serenity. Its divinity keeps me going and believing what I am knowing. Searching for and I always want more, because this thirstiness is as deep as my core.

SIMMER SOUL

Quiet the soul and let it simmer. As you put it on low don't let it dimmer. Let it sit there and know that you have come a long way. And though today is not the day where you will last in one another. At least you have a grasp of one another. More than you had. As much as you started with, but it got lost in the bad and the confusion. You were losing for while but now you are better and you smile in truth. And you have more to lose because you can finally choose. You.

MOTHER

Mama said to never worry. Though the bills were due in a hurry. She said to focus on school. That is what she knew would save us. I use to sleep at night all in fright of what would come. What if, I was not the one to succeed? What if Mama had to plead for us to stay here? Single mother, with myself and my brothers. She stayed strong, making ends meet all along. I use to hear her cry those lonely nights when she missed him. I wondered why she missed him. Leaving such beauty to fend for her duty. Her children of three, I longed for her to feel free of us, her burden, her joy, her earth when...Mama reminded me, not to worry, to enjoy my journey as a woman. I could not help but feel urgency to prove worthy of her. Single mom, so strong all along. I turned snappy. Mom why you always so happy? Your single and do not mingle in the progress. We sit here in the same mess of debt and yet you still have joy. Where did your resilience come from? It must have been made under the sun. Or maybe the moon, in full bloom. Single mother, who looks over me and my brothers. How did you keep calm, when the baby came along and we could not afford anything more. Your beauty is pure. I want to be like mother. Whose core is more gold than the digger. Whose soul has forced me to live bigger. To really see...that love is one single mother.

STUMBLE IN

Sometimes she stumbles, but not only on her words, but on her own crumble. And it is all mix and a mumble when she tries to speak. And as she pleases. She looks to the right but is caught with the leashes. And she stumbles, because now she really is in trouble. As she hopes and prays that no one will see her for days. She is under constant pressure, and she swears it is better than the days there wasn't any. And it's infinity times ten where she feels she has to start over again. But what makes her keep pushing and trying? Though at times she is lying to herself. She doesn't want to ever be put back on the shelf. So she is humble, but from the beginning she starts this mumble of words hoping they would string together, and call on the birds to carry her away. To the furthest sky she can stay. She soars there in earnest heat. Looking to defeat the demons who keep pulling when she's seeking, something more. And at times she is locked in the door. But there is always a way out. And when she finds it there is doubt. But there is light too. And she hopes that she will once again feel true.

YOU BYE GOOD

Truth can come but you cannot. Stay there and think about what you are not. Fulfilling to the nourishment of my soul. So from this moment on it is time to let you go. Go on and get a head start. I will not see you at the finish line. For I have to part ways. And today is the day we say goodbye. I use to kneel to you everyday with a shaky thigh. And a wavering lip. And with eyes that cried for you to go away. And you told me that it was never, and you told me to stay. So I stayed in your presence. I comforted your soul. Though it was sucking my life you refused to let me go. Let's just turn around and forget we knew each other. Skip town and run for cover. I should have never let you in. You almost had the win. And then I realized, that it was my life that had to begin.

Goodbye misery.

SKY TRUTH

Focus more than ever and don't you ever give in. And when they say never begin, they do not know how hard you work, or how much dirt you have dug up just to feel like you can come up and breathe for air. Don't you dare sit there and let them see you bow down. To what is true you are greater than ever. You will see and you will do better. Listen to the sky it does not lie. It opens up your heart so you can finally start your dream. And believe that you can achieve anything. If that is what you want.

ABOVE SUCH

I am starting to see what true light is. Not the one with the switch but the one that hides inside. And that is what I have been searching for. Not the luminosity of the outer but the brightness of the core. The soul, it is there and I feel it inside. And even when I sleep I feel it on my eyes. Shushing me to stop thinking. Shushing me to rest. This inner light only wants me to be my best. And it never goes away, but it sometimes gets dimmer. And that's when I remind myself. I am the sinner who was saved. Who was brave enough to say that is enough I will not take an ounce more of this negative stuff. That comes so often it can be normalized by such. But this true light only emits positive love. And this is the reason I search for above

CHAOTIC PEACE

Peace has come to me at chaotic times. I was sitting there as you were yelling your rhymes. Telling me I had no chance in this life. I should give up now. I could never be a wife. And there in that instant something became still. Something inside, told me that you were just trying to kill out my light. You were nothing but fright and I held this fear too long. So in that moment I was wishing you to be gone. And in that time you looked me in my eyes. And I think you saw my thoughts because you started calling them lies. And I saw the truth right there. It was staring in my face. You never wanted me there. So I moved to discover grace.

ABOUT THE AUTHOR

    Wynter Lauren Eddins is a Spoken Word Artist in Los Angeles. Born in Lancaster, and raised in Los Angles, the city of artistry, Wynter has always been fascinated with the use of language. Her dad encouraged her from an early age to read and memorize portions of the Webster dictionary, which in turn led her to win multiple spelling bees throughout elementary and middle school. Today, she uses her use of language to motivate and inspire others to take risks and conquer their own fears just as she did by conquering her fear of the stage. Since Wynter's performances are the main way she spreads her message, Morph Bred, allows for a wider audience to share with her ideas. With inner strength and faith, Wynter believes anything is possible, and encourages others to use their personal experiences to tap into their unlimited power.

www.ingramcontent.com/pod-product-compliance
Lightning Source LLC
Chambersburg PA
CBHW070457050426
42449CB00012B/3011